Melissa Marie is a mother of two wonderful children, Isabelle and Jean-Luc. She has been married to her high school sweetheart Jean-Alain for 10 years. She is a graduate of Nipissing University where she completed her Bachelor's Degree and Education Degree. She also completed her Early Childhood Education diploma at Centennial College. She is currently a Special Education teacher in Toronto where she loves working with a variety of students who always surprise her with their unique talents and abilities. She loves nature, gardening, reading, and exploring the outdoors with her children.

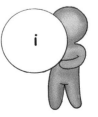

YOU ARE YOU AND YOU ARE GREAT

Melissa Marie

AUSTIN MACAULEY PUBLISHERS™

LONDON * CAMBRIDGE * NEW YORK * SHARJAH

A CIP catalogue record for this title is available from the British Library.

ISBN 9781788787147 (Paperback)
ISBN 9781788787154 (Hardback)
ISBN 9781528955942 (ePub e-book)

www.austinmacauley.co.uk

First Published 2024
Austin Macauley Publishers Ltd®
1 Canada Square
Canary Wharf
London
E14 5AA

To my loving and supportive family, especially Jean-Alain, Isabelle and Jean-Luc.

You were welcomed into the world and made to be great.

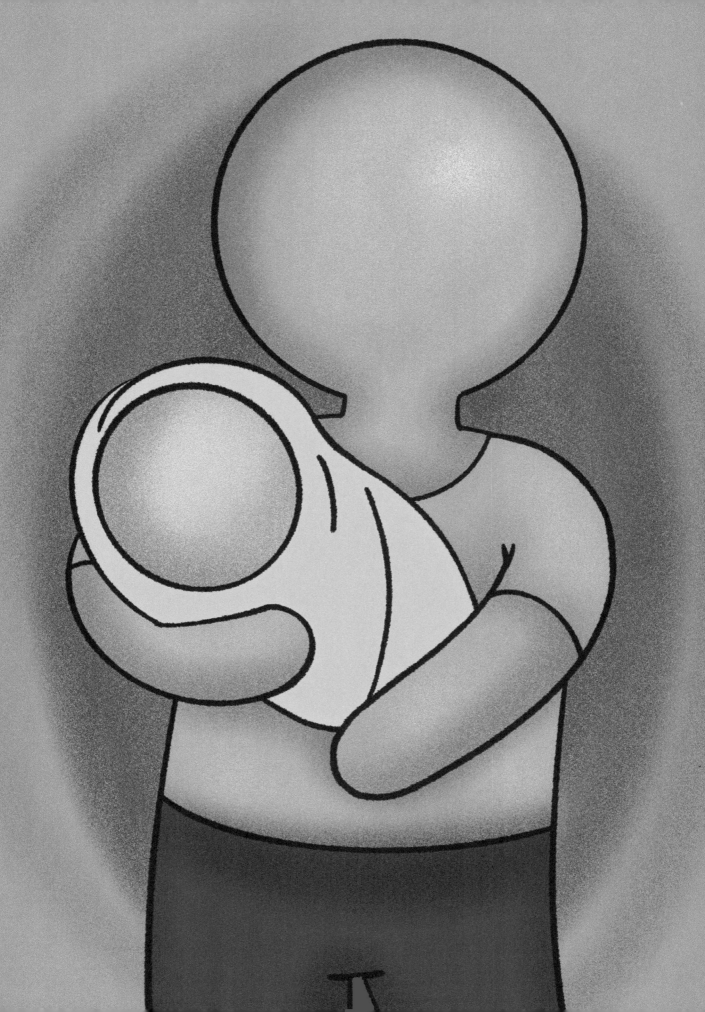

You are special and unique, unlike any other.

You are unique because you have autism.
It has given you gifts
and challenges.

You may see things differently
than others.

You can do things others cannot, try not to get discouraged. You have many people who love you and support you.

You have a team of people to help you and work with you.

The world may seem challenging
or strange.

We will all work together to get through the challenges and difficult times.

We will stay strong and
be successful.

All goals are achievable with hard work and perseverance. You can do what you want and be who you want.

Autism will not hold you back from your goals and dreams. You are you, and you are great.

THE END

Printed in the USA
CPSIA information can be obtained
at www.ICGtesting.com
LVHW062035180524
780463LV00014B/193